Us, then

Us, then

Vincent O'Sullivan

Victoria University Press

TE WHARE WĀNANGA O TE ŪPOKO O TE IKA A MĀUI

VICTORIA
UNIVERSITY OF WELLINGTON

VICTORIA UNIVERSITY PRESS
Victoria University of Wellington
PO Box 600 Wellington
vup.victoria.ac.nz

Copyright © Vincent O'Sullivan 2013
First published 2013

National Library of New Zealand Cataloguing-in-Publication Data

O'Sullivan, Vincent.
Us, then / Vincent O'Sullivan.
ISBN 978-0-86473-892-9
I. Title.
NZ821.2—dc 23

Printed by Printstop, Wellington

For Heidi, John, Dugal

Acknowledgements

Grateful thanks to *Landfall, Listener, Live Lines, New Zealand Books, Otago Daily Times, Peut-être, Sport* and *Warwick Review*, in which some of these poems previously appeared.

Contents

I

II

III

I

According to the doco

Snake-wranglers in Texas hunt the Alamo
for a rattler so huge and mythic
it is called 'The Duke'. It strikes one
on the wrist. Destroys another's fingers.
We're privileged, the wranglers say, that wound
came from The Duke. A celebrated
tracker talks to the camera, he wears
a snakeskin hat made from this critter
went and fanged him twice. Shows his arm,
scoured as if scalded. Tips his hat.
'Mark of respect,' he says. 'You got to respect.'

Speech Day

There is more to the eye than meets it,
as we've always known. Ask the boy
aligning his intended goal, the girl
whose lop-sided bow makes her
yes, perfection! Such fantasy, *enfants,*
in what lies ahead: a knife and fork
to carve the stars.

Getting the picture

(On Barry Cleavin's aquatints, 'Exercising the Black Dog')

The black dog on the street as on the page
  Does as its shadow sets its shape to do,
Each, which claims its role to hold the eye,
  Tempered, observe, by how much light comes through.

Imagine one – you can't – without the other,
  The shadow makes the dog, the dog the dark;
The leash defines what tugs at either end,
  One creature's talk, another creature's bark.

The black dog's questing takes illusion further,
  The sun as megaphone blares time on hold;
The walker and the walked, in pure design,
  The leader and the led mesh as they're told.

The line enclosing both confirms the space
  Light and time and chance neatly permit,
The dog's firm trot, the man's compliant step,
  Entering the instant frame as patterns fit.

'Walking the black dog' as the title says
  Lines up the day, the weather, and two minds;
Shadow and light dependent, each on each,
  We see, half seeing, such shape the image finds.

Words to attend

I like it that Studs Terkel
said as he finished his show
what he picked up from Woody
Guthrie, who used to play it,
'Take it easy, but take it,'
which I'd like to sign off on,
whatever inscriptions are called
if a stone was set up say
with a sentence on it before
as after the song came along.
In another life it might become
a name, that entire sentence,
as Buddhists bestow a new
beginning at the moment breathing
ends, which is yours from now
on, such phrases as 'Dawning
Light', or 'Enduring Peace',
but in this case, this:
'Take it easy, but take it.'
That's the name I'd like.

Cruise ship afternoon

A man of my age sits in a so-so
Dunedin restaurant sipping, I'm guessing,
gin. He wears a tie (it's midsummer),
he's American, his old-fashioned pullover,

his perfectly combed hair, make me
think he must vote Republican in
those marvellous foreign spaces.
I feel the sadness, the distance,

seeping from him, which is high
impertinence on my part. He may own
casinos and the boxing franchise
for Nevada. The mystery never ends.

We will both go out to a late
southern sky, the tail-end of a cyclone
lashing the civic trees Robbie
Burns broods over. One stranger

looks at another. I would have liked
us to talk. At this moment I imagine
he thinks of a woman who may be dead,
as do I of a living woman. How

much goes on behind our fences,
our palisades, our ungift of tongues.
He has paid and left. Now I'm leaving too.
Two worlds gone home.

News from out the Heads

A bereaved albatross, its mate unreturned
from weeks of oceanic scoop and drift,
will up, at some point, relinquish its nest,
go down and join the partying juveniles,
clack beaks, make like its youth again
all over. It seems it works.

I talk with a widowed friend who loathes
heavy metal, rap, facebook, texting.
'I'm too old,' she says, 'to learn not
to spell, to pretend I have never heard decent
music.' Well, I console her, it's hardly
as though you're obliged to assume the skies,
to join the rout. No, she says, but the wind
roars for all that, the sea heaves. It is not
just albatross know about what they've lost.

Against the drift

It was snow falling in streets where snow seldom falls.
It was the sky black as regret and its derisive brawls.
This was the South declaiming, uninvited, on our behalf.
These were the fogged insistent sighs, the iced-rimmed laugh.
This was the Pole's trekked haul, its mounding story.
The yawp of total indifference we grandly took for fury.

If we all went on like this there'd be no stories

'But I said I went into the woods with the rest of the class,'
Belinda (or was it Marjorie? Francesca?) insistently cried.

'There was no boo-hoo from me at the scariest thickets,
no hirsute loon made out he knew Granny,

offered to show the way. No glitter of a vulpine tooth
so much as fancied my apple. I came back. I sat

at the kitchen table, I pressed the four-leaf clover I
found where the paths diverge. When they asked what

else, I said, "But nothing, there was nothing else,
Girl Guide's honour." Not just Da was in a fury.

"That's the last time," my real Gran said, "*you'll* go
into the woods." And my sister seething, "Little slut!"'

What for some it comes down to

Hardly – is that quite the word?
The suicide I am reading would not
have thought so – worth persisting with?
Hardly.

Forever, more tarted up as he
hears it than the fancy announcement
from pediments, fallen temples,
aka, *forever.*

Ramshackle for a while may have served
its turn, the comfort of the pretty
near almost totally clapped out.
Ramshackle.

He went through *his words*, there
weren't so many! Only a dozen, then fewer,
mattered, once the chips were down.
His words

that were then discarded, *put aside*,
this then that, how hollow they
were, the shucks of no longer needed,
put aside.

To *say it*, the last one then,
whatever it was, that last
to be said. All the letters fettered
in one, say. *Say it.*

Cross over, wise guys

The goat looks up and quivers, the calf
tremors its last trot. A knife
tugs its six or seven inches.
Each spasm clinches
those beneficent gods.
The sods.

The historian notes as a matter of course
Caesar from his caparisoned horse
eyeing his priests, concerned
favours are divinely earned,
were it not for that scheist-
er, Christ.

The empire cracked from palaces to huts
like a handful of nuts
crushed by a gladiator
thinking, *Fuck you, frater,*
thinking again, *Ye gods, take cover.*
It's damned near over.

It's each crowned for himself, imperator, comprehend?
It's 'enemy' addressed as 'friend'.
It's every poxed-up face
eligible for grace.
So that's what we're saying, the living end?
Let's not pretend,

this is the instant Jupiter backs down.
'In hoc signo vincis' comes to town.
This is today without tomorrow.
Nothing's left to borrow.
One fact alone to bother.
No bleeding Other.

'Come, you last thing'

Now he was truly burning, the dying
    Rilke said (as though in a hut
the final arsonist laid waste to),

'I will not drag memories inside.'
    One is left, in one's mind at least,
with two piled selves: the ashes

of the blazing shack one
    is resigned to: the perfect untampered
stack, of all left outside.

This time in 3-D

The usual spilling of ten thousand
orcs, the magic swords, dismembered
stacks, a warg's head bouncing the Southern
Alps. A grey unspeakably boring wizard

making his Baden-Powell speeches on keeping
order in the Shire, serving the cause
of peaceable hobbits and shining, pure-
fabricked, waterfall-elegant elves.

I yearn for a piece of human flesh stabbing
for dear life at another piece. I want us
as we've always been. I want Reality
for God's sake, the way it was trickily made!

En famille

I knew a mother and daughter who spoke of little
except umbrellas. I mean, spoke of them together
and felt they were close, as they seldom felt

when it was siblings the child spoke of, or
the mother mentioned X-rays, or the death
of an uncle who ruined himself on horses.

But she phoned this evening from Melbourne –
Mother being in Karori – and she said,
'Today I bought this multi-coloured, *gorgeous*

umbrella at Myer,' and her mother said, 'I remember,
– I can hardly think how far back it was – I bought
an umbrella in Oxford Street made me feel – well – *royal*.'

They laughed. Each said it never occurred as they
shopped whether umbrellas were *functional* –
who'd be so dull! And each felt again

as they placed the phone back in its cradle,
they'd seldom so enjoyed it, talking together, no
mention of fathers, partners, clouds kept at bay.

And

And they stood beside a river so
ordinary that should someone demand
'Think of an ordinary river,' you
might have this in mind, even though
you had never seen it. Thus Plato, he thought,
works on the lowest level, if nowhere else.

She rested her hand on a white wooden
railing, she snapped a dry twig
and both halves bobbed away, as without
the least melancholy she thought
of time passing, she said, 'Why they think
allegory is something *added* on, beats me.'

They said and thought a number of things
determined to distract their minds
from the fact their bodies glanced,
were closer than words might easily say –
touching in fact as if by chance, but
nowhere either admit they'd like them to be.

And he thought, for no appreciable reason,
of a boy thirty years before on a bike
that wobbled badly as it jolted
down summer clay to another
river, where he stood with his line
wound on a stick, swollen as a bandaged

fist it made him think of, then
of the two hooks he took from a Beehive
matchbox, and he thought, 'That's a spider
moving down one knee,' and saw it was
blood from the gorse that whacked him
while the bike jerked on the clay ruts.

And the woman whose book he had thought
was clever, and the woman herself, clever
but so much more, remembered as she
looked at the slow tug of the current
standing in a shallow stream so many
years back, thinking, what will it be like?

And later, my legs still as ugly as this,
just two lines drawn together, I can't
stand seeing them? She slapped a mosquito
that stood on her wet skin, she tasted
the red star it made on the palm
of her hand, her thigh stinging with the slap.

They talk then a little of Woolf, the epi-
phanic tradition, and surprise each
other, surprise themselves, admitting
how Chekov still moves them, naïve
response as that may be – the poignancy,
the achievement, or almost always, the unachieved.

Lake

Loss somehow she always thought of
as a boy entering a lake and both hands
smoothing his hair back after that first
tight-eyed dousing beneath the surface,
and with much more confidence than any swimmer
is ever likely to need, sets off and an hour
later, a dozen searchers scour the beaches,
'a tousle-haired boy' one of them half remembers.
It is still too early to know for certain
yet for certain, nevertheless, known as surely
as salt biting against the wind, the first time
since loss was likely, the taste of the lake.

Nice try

Rasputin handled the soul as a tramp
might finger a carbuncle rubbing the rough
canvas of a shirt he'd flogged from a drunk.
(Russia being not a country so much as a sentence
that goes off and on in various directions.)
Rasputin fed likely followers the line
that without sin, sisters, how can we test
God's love, how know his forgiveness?

He called it a 'Rejoicing',
the chance to sin and so repentance
and so God's hand held out,
the wound in his palm, *voilà,* a little
red gift. 'Help me open his palm,'
Rasputin was inclined to propose.
Can't imagine, can you, saying no to that?
Can't imagine the ice cracking on the coldest night?

Well, not this afternoon

When Zeus looked you could tell
by the stack of ashes
who it was he looked at.

Allah of the unerring sword
spelled a name in quick red
that was lost in no time in the sand.

Yahweh. Now there's a tough
one. A rule for every finger.
Ten reasons to go down.

Sitting beneath a kowhai,
tui flitting their big
blowing cinders –

I don't mind too much
those others haven't made it.
I don't mind that.

Pozo's mate

Jibber, the ambitious critic, clamped between client and clown,
Nicely holding his tongue steady till the master's buttocks settle
   down.

The referees don't mind

how he'd seen no more than a few of her movies, though
it's a timely article to write. He'd forgotten even
watching the most beautiful of drafts blow up
from the grating and that haven for starved mankind
within almost grasp; he'd not read
of the Hollywood ferret by chance encountering
her, naked, in the small hours in a kitchen
and the inevitable bloomed as it has since the sea
gave up its primal whatever-it's-called as he saw
only recently in an Attenborough documentary
when 'The impact of nature narratives' had seemed
a possible topic. But the journal took his paper,
he was home and dozed, as his wife fairly cruelly
put it, knowing his feet were up, his slippers
warmed, if she might venture metaphors which were
not her forte, seeing the article tipped the scales
and tenure was on. His wife in fact who had stood
at a hundred gratings, opened innumerable fridges,
but his name was Stevie and not Frank, and the gown
she donned if going down to the kitchen concealed
completely. Thus props, as he argued, and the adventitious,
shape life as much as art, publish the facts or not.

Some dog

The good bit, she thinks, about
the Tobias story, in his dull enough
duty gathering debts for his dad,
his dodgy make-believe companion,
wings packed in a valise – how
the human is always the fall guy –
is the bit that goes, 'and so the two
went forth, and the young man's
dog went with them.' She likes
that. She thinks of it in the park
walking a red-collared bichon-frise.
An angel. A man who is famous.
Must have been some dog.

Freedom

I miss pure evil.
I miss the hiss when glaring iron
goes dunk into water.

I miss God.
I miss the throat that used
to wear loveliest fogs.

I miss damn all else.
I imagine a straw sucking
colours from whatever else.

Uninvited tribute: eight uneasy pieces

The Christchurch earthquake, and reading Terry Sturm, again brought to mind the importance of Lyttelton in Curnow's biography, and its resonances in his poetry. So much of his work considers the tracking of time and its drum-beat conclusion, as it quarries threat and apprehension and self-defining; and builds on that cleared space of what Anglicanism had meant to him, and what its language continued to bear once doctrine lost purchase. I remember a story told to me by Fred Page, pianist and professor, brother of the famous cricketer 'Curly' Page. Fred was a schoolmate of Curnow's in Lyttelton, where his father was a coal merchant. He recalled Allen's early shame, when he once came to school without shoes. Rightly or wrongly, I cannot help but relate that anecdote to Curnow's prickliness and pride, both inseparable from his qualities as a poet. Recent photographs of his father's shattered church, and the fractured remains of 'the time-ball' tower which survive in the poetry, are vivid reminders of the boyhood world Curnow circled in numerous ways. The poems I call 'Uninvited Tribute' are a kind of homage to a not altogether likeable man (I knew him only slightly), but our finest poet. I suspect he may have regarded anything so unrequested as an impertinence, especially as much of their imagery purposely derives from his own.

1
Blood clouding (by rumour) the lipped chalice,
salting (taste it!) the broad bay's shelving off,

brimming too the victim's eye with west's
impending wrack, shadows silked as

te mako's cruising, closer in by far.

Pretty much, pretty much as is,
the refrain falling as a flung stick
for a bitch's late run morsing
the beach's narrowing stretch,
                              belling vespers'
high memo, as Father once lofted
    Lessons, boy, to be learned!

2
Raised
tall as talked-up tallness
in the child's knee-high version

the Author of all clenched close
as a favourite marble

ancestors loading the skyline
at ease as stone.
What you touch is what you
fathom
        what you see
is the eye opening, radiant
paddocks otherwise special
                    than in scything hymns.

The harbour's bright bill of lading
taking time on tick.

3

And spring, let the season
spare the boy's bare-heeled
bracing of cold in Lyttelton
shame as Fred Page read
it, church-poor and poorer
than the coalyard's brothers,
the cricketer, the pianist,
who at least clanged boots.
                              Bells
though tempered nicely
given time, given times,
the boy's to the end and beyond
good as newly rung.
                              Young
Page insisting, 'Vain
at that age even,' playgrounds
reminisced, the iron-clappered
pealing from father & Father
to ensuing sons.
                    The steeple
on course to be fractured,
the time-ball crazed.
And the shock of the poems,
writes Allen,
                    scores still to come.

4

A wet wind rumours the macrocarpa
proposing nothing but itself.
                              A branch cracks.
A bird's damp *flut*. Light
talks through rain.
                    Much as pyramids,
as duomos, up to the same lurk, wind
urging on,
              the instant barked to heel.
                                    'Maestro
to the pit' as they call at the Met,
awaiting the beat, assuming *il mondo
magnifico*'s scoring, delivering time.

5
'Not a nice lad, especially.'
                              So?
The boy unpacking language, his special meccano,
flexing the big tin pieces, defting tiny screws.
'See what I build for myself' is the morning's news.
A which is his to begin with, down to Z in tow.

6

As Stevens your closest wordmate plied you,
'There is no such thing as innocence in autumn.'
The old labels float, the brand names wear.

Poets inclining, picturesquely, to scuff at leaves,
call variants of red by their variable names,
testing the touch of what remains in mind,

'words to enflame,' as he says, the fun of the phrase
refuting the by-heart preacher, 'This takes care of time.'
One spark feeding another, the point of rhyme.

7

The cliff face bleeds, the wound is personal.
The slaughtering wrist aches with expertise.

Myth slips its scarlet needles to the harbour's vein.
The business of breath catches at vacated space.

How a late stroll to the west shoulders sharking dark.
How the whole damned empyrean makes its move!

8

Homage:

      as if you'd have tossed it
a second word, as if privacy wasn't
bunkered in each public stanza,
as if nailing as good as a century
with the scorer's crest

                wasn't tribute drilled
from the only well that pays:

              as if *Self*
spelled out in increasing type
hadn't pressed you as surrogate Adam,
the one world launched to a tongue's fathom,
on cue each calling

        necessary once named.

II

Screensaver

I am a grandfather in this photo,
I am holding a year-old child.
As you'd expect, at my age,
he is made of gold.

This is Boxing Day, Cessnock,
in the Hunter Valley. Moths
pelt the screens. A thin rain
grazes the blue trees.

Reflection, this time of night,
slips, thank God, to clichés,
an aging man, a child who
may never know him.

Nothing to regret, neither weather
nor place, neither time nor distance.
This is where we are, eh Joey?
The luck of that.

Road from the Camp

A story here I wish I hadn't heard –
a row of prisoners stitched with yellow stars
marching a summer road, oddly surprised
to pass a compound lined with circus bears,

with creatures of diverse and mottled kind,
remnants from simple entertainments lost.
Both sides look up, confused, the memories stir,
the bears perform their stunts for favours tossed

once their way by children, parents – scraps
for begging paws. Those mimed displays
a hundred years back, was it? Thinking how
they and these once met in civil ways.

This is the story of the final show,
the trawl of stars from village and from city.
The bears withdraw their paws, conclude their dance,
watching the humans pass with almost pity.

That time of year

Bonhoeffer's Xmas trees, falling,
falling still,
                         seventy years after,
who's to deny their thrill?
The branches that transfigure, the branches
that brightly kill?

Dead priest, in what we presume
your total dark,
                         your hoping to rake
from cinders some preserving spark –
Lord, this salvation's racket
a rare old lark!

Each nail in its promised shudder
making its point,
                         this moment the one
and only, the wired, wary saint
taking in the tree, the fall,
the believer's faint

insistence, *this is never all,*
incendiary grace
                         flaring the edges,
the centre, the appointed place,
the turning to face the wall,
the allotted space.

Kafka and Christ in cahoots
dispute together
                         the raging of light,
the mind's wildest weather,
stories of endured breath,
death's unmoved feather.

Note: As Geoffrey Hill recalls in his poem on Dietrich Bonhoeffer, the German Protestant cleric executed in 1945, incendiary bombs were known by locals as 'Christmas trees'.

The problem of style

'The cold music of longing' someone writes.
I do not believe him. 'An ice-sheet
of desire,' he might as well say, 'A cauldron
of frozen cubes.' There is longing or there
is not. No one camps on an outcrop
which is in between, or neither.

                                      'Hell's hot gates'
as a friend once put it to me, slightly overstated,
as so much that may be worth saying so
inevitably is. But we knew at once, our parched
throats, sweat flooding our eyes, we
knew without needing to clamber the crater's
rim, we knew from the haggard faces
of those making it back.

                              So again, as again,
that 'music of longing', the romantic chords,
the frenetic brass, the circle, as Dante swirled
it, whirling bitter flakes – 'longing'
poured simple as that, the old metaphors
brittle as snake casts once they're said.

Imago: Three

1

Before Darwin, for example,
you could scarcely think swan
without thinking mirror, mirror
without gliding, glide and the soul
feathered in there somewhere,
'classical' we called it, the crystal
picture reflecting superbly, *O bella
figura,* take me home!

2

A road between mountains that edge in
close as cats.
          The sky clawed
at their rising.
               Stroked tussock purrs.

3

More the fountain lifts
               more
its falling back, its calling –
Narcissus in high delight
curves his slender waist,
               back,
always back, the promise –
so much more the same!

On the pleasure of former colleagues

We order another bottle, there is so
much more for me to hear.
'Where was I?' he says, eyeing the label
carefully, nosing the glass.
'The third opera,' I remind him,
the third opera he was fortunate enough
to take in on his way *back*
from Bayreuth. 'Dear old Verdi,'
he chuckles, 'he still pulls them in.'
He edges aside his books about
the death of a guru journo,
a witty monograph on Proust.
He laces his fingers so very like
an interesting cleric who has, believe
me, a lot you'll be more than glad
to attend.
          I think of a big brass vase
I saw in a museum, aeons of verdigris
thickening still on one side, the other
dipped and scoured, drinking the sunlight
from a nearby window, as though
there might never be enough of it, sunlight.
I face my friend and listen and wish
I could turn the vase a little
so that not only the green mould
faced me, those centuries of accumulated
culture, but the merest glimpse,
even that would suffice,
of the bright fat cheek of the early
objet, before the smear on
one's fingers at the slightest rub.

Spacing out, they will tell you

She said, 'I am sorry I have nothing more to take
off,' when she stood, stark as a lightbulb,
because, as she knew, even her famous bosom
could make the tongue in his mouth wrench about
like a suddenly waterless fish. 'Because,'
as she also confided, 'I fully intend
to excite you beyond the point of likely survival.'

'Done,' he said. Then, 'Only for you I'd propose
to proceed with a blindfold angled across
my eyes, the one way I might thank you,
Liebling, for such palpable craft.'

So they bounded away on the erotic highway,
felt galaxies slip the horizon,
lovely silver shoals. By the time indeed
their arms flung out in the usual panting
posture of human limitation, he opened
his eyes, *even then,* and metaphors
lost any sense of precedence completely,
and crowded the room like, so he wryly
put it, like he didn't know what.

The story, as they realised then and corrected
in proof, did not initiate there nor did it end.
Cosmonauts, as they like to say, are scarcely confined
by timing from mundane downtown earthly clocks.

What's it called, again?

I'd not known their name for years –
three trinity-like petals, three within those,
tigered, flecked.
                      Then today they're named –
Peruvian lilies, lilies of the Incas.
                                There's a posher name.
Linnaeus who labelled them first
remembered, 'Ah! My friend the Baron
von Alstroemer. Give my mate a bloom.'

That's a pedigree to cope with,
this table-clutch of fine-lined trumpets,
leaves curiously twirled. ('Resupinate'
should you ever need it, the bottom of leaves
turned uppermost, the top beneath.)

'Inca lilies' does for us.

No longer listed

They were so colourful these two,
so heavily apart, I think of them
still as I look at a Tiffany
lamp,
    lead seeming to be
what makes them, so defining
the brilliance, one pane
set against another: my dear
lead friends, I call them,
light strews through both.

Infra-red

or whatever one calls it, that greenish light where the secrets
happen in the smuggled News? The night time obsequies,
the early hours' slaughter?
                   A man carries his daughter for burial,
she is like a Xmas ham in her gauzed smallness.
A woman shouts at the camera, we feel good as she's
translated, 'Freedom!' she shrieks, we cosily admire
her shouting, a smear of blood along her side where
she ran her hand after touching the body that makes
her shriek. The wobbly green light finds another
target. He bleeds into his beard. He wears pure
white, like an apparition, the headband on the chequered
squares perfectly in place: all this on the News!

We come out from the weird light to the reach of day,
to the nasty colours in the makeshift wards, a boy
with a thumbprint of blood on his fractured glasses,
his throat dragged back.
                  Like that piece of meat carried in
at Xmas, that's all I can think of, that as I know
is not what I should think, the father wading
the green shadows, the distorted light, there must be
somewhere, the girl's father believes, somewhere
he can lay her down, let her not be touched.

'Only connect'

Opening 'LinkedIn' I'm delighted – again – to note:
Lydia Sparrow is now connected to David Branch.
Eric McFinger is now connected to Tane Lim.
Debbie Seacliffe is now connected to Janet Frame.
The promise is endless. Gabriel is now connected
to the Virgin Mary. The Führer is now connected
to Josef Goebbels. Lucifer would like to be
connected to any of the above. 'Arsebook'
is now connected, momentarily, to 'Facebook'.
What a wonderful world.

Still

There's that friend, remember, who says, 'Living
is finally what we do about it' –

calling the midwife, ensuring a theorem
is learned by heart, wanting to know
exactly what constellation glitters
through the square of fanlight in the old
kitchen in a back-country shack.
It comes down to that.

                    To what
we are left with when the credits
scroll as a rule too quickly,
flash too simply, one's dying
to know who played me, the man
one has almost been, at least
in that other epic, the one whose
script one implied if not performed –
the man who picks off the copper-
heads at twenty paces, the Armani
cuffs at another locale, lord of
visible realms . . .

                    And today when I've heard
a man as dear as any is due to be
dead within months, the amber light
as they say already slowing the traffic,
the clap-board, assuming another image,
snaps down, 'Final Take' . . .

                    The heat storm
hassles the late sky, the bears
he delighted in still nosing the berries,
the bats on another coast streaking their
millions, trailing a brown river,
their rustling dense as blood cells.

The same, we would like to say, evening
after evening, even now with stark
branches in depleted months, the fruit
whose drench we find it hard to imagine,
yet to say it, still, *evening after evening,*
the bats now draped in their racks, the bears
pawing ice, *evening after evening:*
skies empty as film once lighting fails.

Act V

The ice shrinks,
The sea rises,
The God who does not
Persist, despises.
The song runs out.
There are no reprises.

From the 'Culture' column

It's a sad enough story, the woman said
who told me about a writer – or a painter, was it? –
who never had quite the luck or the skill or the right
friends to make it, working so honestly,
diligently, without achieving; not a cell in his body
she said even fringing on malice, envy, plagiarism,
what have you. His abiding eccentricity his knack
to leave umbrellas anywhere he went – cafés,
girlfriends', buses, opera stalls, a church.
His pictures – or stories, was it? – not so much forgotten,
'forgotten' meaning once admired but now
like most of art quietly, painlessly replaced –
but stolidly unheard of from the morning
they were done. Yet nose around, fetch his collected
horde of brollies, you could mount a show. She herself
had one, the woman said, blue, a leather
duck-beaked handle, left at her place from a party
circa '84. A friend had told her of a husband
who had two. In an age of alert curators
with an eye for a break, *The Dream of Imminent Rain*
could be in for a more than timely *vernissage*.

What men envy most

The nice thing about her favourite singer
  said the lady behind the counter
was the kitchen at home lit up like a liner
when she joined in with 'Amore' or whatever.

Where my breath lurches as my crooner sings
  said the woman at Weight Watchers
is at how the same old kitchen rings
as I cook yet again my favourite things.

The scale for me that I like to catch
  said the home-bound slapper,
is the one that strikes me a dangerous match,
so the kitchen burns down to a flaring patch.

When we descant together how we raise the tone
  throat the three-in-one chorus,
raise the brim of contentment to a nicely moan,
a garden of herbs where the weeds had grown,
  sing the women now as the women before us,
  not giving a toss how the neighbours' dogs deplore us.

Trade aid

A week of builders, plumbers, electricians,
brings home for the hundredth time
how skills of such kind are for real,

while I browse a collection of reviews
that make embarrassment a luxury,
their arch-importance rising from the pages,

so I think of a skinny busker with a bamboo
flute forty years back close to Leicester
Square, raising a drugged snake from a basket,

and a copper, weary and patient from all he
has seen, telling him, 'Here, just put that snake away!'
I hear the honest banging of the men on the roof.

When, exactly?

It was a curious thing, in a Waikato paddock,
a day when wind seemed a story you had half-
forgotten, the puriri's every twig as though carved
from jade, the late corn squadroned in the paddock
you stood in.
        In the 3 o'clock steaming silence
you could hear the minute rustling of jaws – 'Army
worm' they were called, taking their luck, their
time, on the uncut crop. It was hearing yourself
age. It was *here,* surrounded by before and after,
yet moving, moving, at the pace of an insect set
against ten hectares. It was summer, 1968.

What story's that, then?

Mice big as teapots come into a story
I overhear a mother reading to a child on the bus
along Musselburgh Rise. The child,
a finger stuck for the last few minutes
in one nostril, is past boredom. She detests
the mice, the ridiculousness of teapots.
I don't hear what else is in the story,
presumably worse, the child now crying
at the insult to reality she is expected
to attend. Then a dog, a greyhound,
skinny as a one-line drawing of a dog,
is on the crossing near Countdown with a woman
whose ambition, you might say about her
in a story, was to be a ball, and in time
to roll rather than waddle. Its collar is studded
with fake gems, its lead lolly pink.
The dog looks as if he hates it. The child
is elated. Both hands make squashy stars pressed
on the window. 'God,' she says, 'God,' and the mother,
embarrassed in front of the two women and the one
other man on the bus besides the driver and myself,
says loudly, 'Doggie, doggie,' but the child is grinning
from there into town. She has seen the world, and named it.

After reading the warnings

So kissing as they now say was tonguing
an ashtray. Her fingers dabbled tar since Third
Form. Her hair when you pressed against it
made you think of curtains in a room
where smokers had raddled their lungs
for a generation. I know that. I agree
as the nurse aid scours the very air
so we thrive on an atmosphere before sin
was packaged. She asks my age and I
smile, 'The one thing I hope to forget
and damn me, Sister, it's the one thing
I can't.' (She likes that 'Sister', the instant
promotion.) And 'of course,' I say, 'of
course,' with the certainty of saying 'God'
or 'Not long now' or 'The sun skidding
the harbour makes the day worthwhile';
or better, what else I think of, could never
not think of, the slope we walked
above the suburban streets to the stand
of pines we fancied were ours, especially,
and the way words simply weren't up
to what we had to say to each other,
and 'beauty' didn't half do justice
to your hair handled by the wind, your
throat was a place I tried to say I'd
start building a temple; and coming back,
always, you'd say, 'My God, I've earned it,'
and light up. As you still do, light up,
against the dark. Notwithstanding warnings.

Road

In almost a last letter Stevens writes
'The peonies have just opened', a letter
that stuns for its directness.
                              Peonies
opening as the world has always
opened, *This is today, this*
is what today so abundantly is
elsewhere, even as imagined.
                              Fact driving into
poetry, poetry into fact,
as headlights towards a hospital
some ordinary evening, efflorescing,
white such final bloom.

Listen, this isn't easy

In a street the experts say will be the first
to fall completely once hit, let's say, by a force
6, accepting the fault's as close as they know
it is, he watches the woman across the table

as they cover the old ground, the politics,
the nastiness, the rare gold threads in
the seam. They say, That was it, all right,
knowing, Not quite. They make allowances

for age, for time. They joke, without saying
a word on the rust that has run the guttering,
the eaves, the borer in the wooden
joists, the fracturing between the bricks.

You are still lovely, he wants to say, although
saying as much would make the evening unlovely.
You are excellent and courageous, he could
tell her, but quite rightly does not. They know

what carefully to avoid, as Marines in movies
skirt the living, expectant fields. They carry
the white flags both sides accept. In the sun,
this late in the story, red at any distance.

On the track above the bay

Grinning was the best part of it,
once you'd scoffed the blackberries
up above the beach:
                              you grinned black
like a crazed ink-drinker,
                              well,
rusted ink, let's say:
                         an elderly
man who had eaten libraries
liked watching the child:
                              'Some
taste bitter, or better than others,
you'll never run out', though
scratches along her arms'll tell him
how 'Hard to get at them, see, my wrists
still bleeding'.
                  It's red scribble, she thinks
of. Or 'Like lace', he wants to tell her,
'like stinging lace'.

Ciao!

I don't like it that the undertaker
hands round a basket of flowers
so we drop something we haven't grown
or even picked ourselves on an old
mate as still as he'll ever be
while the hot-house carnations
pitter patter, everything made so *nice*.

He, like pretty much anyone
you might think of, ran with bare
feet as a child, felt dirt
on his hands as he grew older
and there was nothing much he finally
valued that couldn't be summed
up in a phrase like, 'The earth,

and what it's good for', which
fairly much covers the lot.
So I'd sign a petition any day,
march up and down church aisles
for whatever government brought it back –
the gritty handful as you lean towards
him, its last exultant thud.

Stop it now, can't you?

The arm twists. The skin burns.
'No, never. Not once! I'm prepared
to sign! It was never Art I wrote for!'

Another takes the probe.
'For love then, was it?' 'Christ, no!
Never a line of mine reached far as another!'

He greets weakly, now it's third degree.
'What? To improve the world? Patriots?
Workers? Pluck an eye if I did!'

'There,' the interrogators agree, 'give
the man a scotch. Though disappointing,' they
chide, 'how even under duress you told the truth.'

Nowhere further from Belgium

My grandmother used to say
'Just do your best now'
when a drawing came out smudgy,
a list of words for spelling
crossed out here and there.

I thought of that this morning
when the sea at Orepuki
banged like a hundred bibles
angrily shut, a place
no more this morning

than its few dead shops, a pub,
a maimed main street, a cemetery
on a dirt road and a white
blunt column among local
graves; a boy it remembers,

someone's boy in his early
twenties, dead somewhere
in Belgium, where bits
of the distant boy were gathered,
one hopes, by mates.

One thinks of him here, 'signed up',
his spruce regimental number
in the street where so much happened,
a uniform doing wonders
whatever the wind, the sea,

the sand graining the text
on the marble plinth, his telling
the girls, 'Yeah, try to do
my best', his cobbers' pissed
shiyacking, 'Glamorous bugger!'

The incentives, south

I read a poem in which clouds travel
overhead to Bergamo, Padua, presumably
further than that – Pompeii, Etna,
Sicily's sprawl – nowhere being out of the question
once you look up in Europe and take in
a cloud. You will always be somewhere
this time tomorrow that reeks of battles,
duomos, canvases, vileness, pure glory.

After I close the book with admiration
and envy, I watch our sky crumble
and fragment from the north, pour its embassies,
argosies – one chatters the chat
of magnificoes once it's cloud you're into –
which will float, will steer above emptiness,
stark drear, not a resonant name
you'll salute between here and the Pole;

coasts scoured by meagre reference,
sheer, unvisited fjords,
the seas whose dead, even those,
are numbered at most in dozens –
then the globe's tilting to final whiteness
you fail to imagine, those skies you have
lost completely. You are left with facts,
not words. Clouds without Bergamo.

Always on the cards

I haven't been to Karachi. I've imagined it though.
I know they have problems there, and marriages
arranged by dealers, much as cricket matches
might be arranged. I know there are streets
more colourful than I'm likely to comprehend. There
are beautiful children with eyes no tourist's
camera could resist, beautiful hungry children.
But that's by the bye. I'm trying to find some
way to think of being dead, and it seemed
not too absurd to consider it merely a place
I've never arrived at, but when I'm there, all I'm
used to goes on back here as it does, this minute
if you like, a car-horn jammed in a garage
round the corner, the heater I'm anxious if it's been
turned off, a book with a bookmark's lolling
leather tongue. It's a matter of travel,
to put it blandly. Have you been dead lately?
I imagine someone saying, and answering, No,
but I still intend to, as I hope to visit Karachi.

Loose change

1
It was another day so similar to this,
how is one so sure each is not the same?
I'll tell you how. One tilts towards the other
the way a candle tilts to share a flame.

2
There's a picture on the museum pad I'm using,
a reproduction of Ingres' naked odalisque.
Should you flick the pages quickly there's more
than eighty stirring, putting the town at risk.

3
We used to argue so much about a dog
we loved, we traded him in for a cat we loathed.
Unanimity settled like a perfectly fitted hat.
The purest loves are often unhappiest clothed.

4
The sun as everyone says sets later
the longer the day persists.
'The majority are right even when they're fools,'
the blind democrat insists.

5
The vainest writer I knew thought earthly fame
his likeliest option, then hedged his bet
on hearing it rumoured that the Trinity
was expanding to a Quartet.

6
In Poussin's *Extreme Unction* grief tremors
from pallid forehead to chrismed foot.
Eleven are caught in sorrow – bar the exiting maid,
fleshy as sunlight, knowing you know she's a beaut.

7

Philosophy some patsy tries to put across
is laughter confronted by the void.
Hence the leathery misery one supposes of libraries?
The sly beetle in the wood?

8

I put down Plato and watch Astaire,
the soft shuffle, the definitive tap.
Life's a pretty short boardwalk, partner.
Someone's got to take the rap.

9

Giraffes belting hell from each other,
challenged by an even deeper throat.
Any wonder missionaries cried
in Edenic horror, '*Ach, mein Gott!*'

10

'And regrets?' A war reporter
quizzing Achilles in his tent.
'Sure there are, buster. Should have
dragged him round Troy again before I went.'

11

New lovers tapping at windows, bolting sudden doors,
could the heart after all accept anything but surprise?
The view she's accustomed to not worth a toss
the moment an unknown hand slips across her eyes.

12

Hear them, the trade winds electric in the palms,
the great jerked spiders clawing the coasts.
An image that dies quick as the click of a watch.
In a second, still, stiller than concrete posts.

13

'Among the great poets after my death' – Keats
coping with genius, with despair.
'Oh, sooner than that,' whinnies our prancing local,
'soon after breakfast actually *I'll* be there.'

14

The sweat shops of India make our day,
Nike piles its millions on a swinging stick.
We cheer. We holler. We slobber to fill the tills.
Crave poverty's priceless tick.

15

'Pogrom' unsettles whenever I see it,
as if something I fear in the dark back of a cage.
It is not the sound of marching, it's the silence.
And the silence following the silence, as you turn the page.

16

It wasn't the burned tents he feared most,
or even survival against the odds.
It was how they would be there, bright as ever,
as if it hadn't concerned them, the household gods.

17

'When I'm really in love,' she says, 'I'm like
some scene in Hitchcock, only nicer birds
and no knives!' 'You won't like the knives,'
he tells her, 'once the birds hear that!'

III

Guests are invited to consider

That one may be shelved next to McGonagall,
That not all tweed is from Donegal,
That love may on occasion be a bit of a have,
Everest a drawing on the wall of a cave.

Even so, one takes the risk to rhyme,
To wear one's jacket, stamp love's flank with 'Prime',
Look from the window and think, 'Just the day for a climb.'

St Clair, September

The sea, this first day of spring – what
ever message it carries beached as
distant whiteness, the diminishing South,
its slipped plateaux, its fractured
bergs, sluicing to tell us something
we are learning, just, to hear.
                                   'We are meant
to be its confrère,' the loon on the sand
interprets for us, the tilt of gulls
against the wind etch calligraphies
of their own.
                    As ever, as ever,
the surf insisting its rewrite, tide too
a word that will have to learn to change,
to reconfigure, as the swift edging gulls
into altered air.
                       The loping loon
at St Clair froths a little as he tells
you, his eyes slightly scary as eyes
are, knowing they're right: 'I'd ring,' he
says, 'the shark-bell but the rope's been flogged.'

As the boy, the man

Clean cuffs, as always insisted his doting mother,
the essential courtesy you pay the other

person you speak with, instruct, or indeed obey.
Dirty shoes, on the contrary, presage a dirty day.

So a smile in consequence was what he wore
whether to headmaster, maître d', or whore.

Whether a man was worth a farthing or a million or two,
his manner never faltered, thanks were always due.

A kindly word, the occasional intimate song,
quite usefully eased the line between right and wrong.

It was possible, he found, to make quite a mess
of a woman's future by complimenting her dress,

as possible as he had learned deftly to sink
well-holes in a gullible fortune over a drink.

So a smile and shiny shoes and ten well-clipped nails
carried him high as the kite of fortune sails.

And when things turned bad and the famous army failed
he took as politely all that the loss entailed.

He thanked the judge and tipped the unpleasant gaoler.
He patted the shoulder of the wooden overcoat's tailor.

He bowed to the squad who'd fire then have to lug it.
As his last request he asked simply, 'A spot of Nugget.'

His batman permitted even to press his shroud.
Happy the man whose last word, 'I know mother's proud.'

Fine distinctions

There is a certain tedium in fine distinctions,
in Wittgenstein, to take a handy instance, considering
the choice of dimensions for an imagined bridge.

Imagining's burden, if one might call it that,
is to have one declare, with certainty, how
imagining works through to reality's end.

But what, one might then insist, have I actually
achieved? – 'justified the choice of dimensions for
a bridge', or merely, an *imagined* choice been

made for an *imagined* bridge? – not by any leap
the same, though mind's seduction for the moment
lazily claims, *They are.* The question is posed,

the answer left to what may be, but never is,
called the questionee? A strange word for the occasion,
clarity wrecking confusion, the bridge brought down.

Nothing truer, mind

Remember the Frenchman who said philosophy
– or one philosopher, at least – had cut
poetry's throat? The man casually beneath
the blue tree holding the white book
doesn't mind that the Frenchman said so.
He as casually liked it that he did.
He liked it, the featured poet's
throat a child might gruesomely draw
so it seemed a red ship sailing
from ear to ear, or a skipping–rope
dipped in paint and cleverly caught
at the very grinningest part of its
swing in the shouting playground . . .
Yes, he liked it, the reading man
with the white book in the yellow field.
Unless the Frenchman had told us
you'd fancy philosophy had so little
to offer poetry, philosophers solemnly
stropping razors for pure fun.

Closer though than one might think

'That hurt?' asked the self who fancies
   dreamwork carries its slivered diamond,
      what we may as well call truth.

'That hurt?', teeth biting the thin
   wire ring that shocks her nipple,
      and 'Sure,' she says, 'what else do you think

it's there for?' She smiles like someone
   I once knew who's been dead for years,
      who died where she planned to die in the Blue

Mountains, a place where boredom, which was
   always a problem, turned insistently dark,
      no door was left worth opening apart from one

she decided to leave shut. She could smile
   and her eyes regret it in the middle of parties
      she had no vocation for, I remember that,

a non-believer in the music was rumoured
   to set you down, in fact was putting
      couples down all round us, at the glittered

palms, the curved samurai-sword beaches
   the next song offered if the last didn't
      deliver. Why this dream though now

one's a little ashamed of? 'Nothing like either
   of us,' one's obliged to say a few minutes
      later, the sun stalking the edge of a dark

ceramic bowl on the sill, light's mildly
   sinister insect slipping this way and that
      should you move your head, even slightly.

Someone at a reunion told me that,
    more than a decade later, about the town
        with its dense eccentric gums, the vistas blue

with eucalypt vapour, where you came to calling
    it quits. 'No, I'll see you there,' was the last
        thing she had once told me, or something like

it, meaning a student party she didn't get to.
    'Did that hurt?' as I've just asked her
        in that dream of what never almost happened.

But I like her answer. I like the no-nonsense
    of it, the way there's no way to make it
        come across as nice, now Robin's dead.

Madame takes a third ouzo

The mirror is mounting one of its wicked stories,
the river springing at her its tireless flash.
'Snow Black!' tittles one of her down-at-heel fairies
who lisped as a child, confusing 'God' with 'Oh, gosh!'

The mirrors and the rivers prattle regardless,
the banks framed chocker with believing folk;
the purest tongue has been known to slaver at arse,
the eighth corporal work of mercy a digital shock.

How the wise man wisely stands at the brimming mirror
how the picture-book raven croaks to the talkative river
how the dullest girl in the class contrives something clever
as Mr Kurtz cuts it short, his yelp about horror.

Then the river kindly reflects as the mirror assures,
words may be doused in both and the image survives.
'Cracked as intended' the glass now amusingly purrs.
Niagara smartly curves its cold steaming knives.

Come September

The last, the latest, of alterations have begun
again, the boxed earth at the side of
the steps talking sudden spring;

where the frost held the shallow bird-bath
in its thick-thumbed grip, a blackbird scatters
dollops against the fence;

the dead coiled wire flares its hoops,
forsythia's dozened matches spluttered back.
An accustomed woman enters

a cold room, smiling, the room is a different
precinct, with different names. And so it goes.
'What was that?' we try

to remember, before the windows could be left
open, before branches fuzzed the star that had stood
naked, until this week –

when was that, those far mornings we thought,
'This time the word somehow has not got through' –
the crocuses though as ever in the know.

Matched up

Her leaning half-way behind a door
so it was half of her, he used to say,
he so fell in love with. 'To have
loved you all,' he assured, 'would have
been to jump on the pyre completely,
I doubt I'd have survived it!'

A Picasso moment with a vengeance –
one eye to stand in for both, one breast
like a circle a mathematician might
instruct on for half an hour. 'No one
is ever perceived completely' – that,
don't we know it, is lesson one.

This hint too of Plato's warehouse,
he's inclined to say of that half
he does not take in entirely, aspects
not here yet always there. 'So belief is
putting together whatever is, whenever?'
'That's for real,' he'll tell you.

He discourses on. Her scissors
click along the table to the pattern
she devises. 'Flimsy now,' she announces
as she drapes its tissue against her,
'come back after lunch the fabric'll
hold its own.' He expounds,

she scissors precisely; he figures
tomorrow's the likeliest time to observe,
she puts it more precisely, 'About three.
By then the bread's baked as well.'
He gifts her the half door for her
to lean on. She's there, without the door.

Random as

it struck him, the bike with its handlebars tipped
up, the way it lay there in the long grass
as a kind of creature that could at any moment
get to its knees, its horns dip towards him.

It seemed beyond making sense, as did
two grown-ups that other day in the woods
pretending to help with putting each other's clothes
on, wanting him to believe that's what they were at.

A friend he liked at school was sent to another
school, it was in the papers, the cat he tied
to the rails so a train would get it only a man
saved it, was what his own mother called
a hero, the same man who did things in the sheds
kids knew about, though not their parents.
'Saved by a whisker' the newspaper said.

Matters of perspective, as we learn to say,
so summer is neither short nor prolonged,
room temperature is a matter of taste,
the person you like most to walk with in the evening
is by the river where you know a fish leaps
by the rings that expand only once it has leapt.
Enough of those he comes to consider suffice
for a life story, rings becoming a chain.

There's a one-legged starling, crikey, hardly holds the wire!

Not included in the footnotes

A thing to confess, to have sat here at my age,
a Catholic as much by repute as by mundane choice,
craving to shelter from rain in Knox's church,
Dunedin – grey as thinking grey on the greyest day,

grateful to stone-jawed Reverend Stuart on his plinth
at the side of the church, my assuming his brow
in itself enough to harden local granite.
And to read, for the first time, that ripping yarn,

the *Book of Joshua* until the rain's eased off
like fingers that insist then decide to relent.
And how detestable I find him – not Joshua, only,
so proud of his badges, thumbing his diligent

sword, flushing out back-sliders, but
the Merciless Presence too commanding his heart,
so chuffed at how Jericho fell to the old oom-pah,
how its families were scraped, disposed of, dog-shit

from his shoe. And the one man I care for, the one
I would like to meet, Achan who fancied 'a goodly
Babylonish garment' as the city was sacked –
something in the cut, I suppose, the weave, the *beauty*,

that abandoned word. Achan who could not accept
Verboten once glamour flared him beyond
the rules. This late in the day, less use, I know,
than the finch's tiny feather on the sill beside me,

yet still, I insist, 'Achan, I'm glad you kept it,
the lovely cloak. You are more to me than
the Reverend Stuart even on his marble stand,
than Joshua swooping nastily down on Canaan,

Yahweh's dripping hawk; than the Big Gun
behind him, a voice like Kalashnikovs riddling a village.
I would like you to shelter here too, in Dunedin rain.
You could share my coat, Achan, which is not forbidden.

Puritan Sunday

Listen, if poetry's denied its odd flashy dollop,
its swiney snout, its lick at the jewel–
hung ear,
        if the shelves in the kitchen are to be
arranged with the labels always neatly printed,
both myrrh and arsenic forbidden substances,
the glass-case locked with its glinty sequins,
the Coronation clackers, the sentimental
mementoes grubbed with thumbs,
                then count me out.
Memory's a mangy mount for sure, yet hey!
its trot urges cornettos as the joust
begins; a brilliant late cut struck to an opened
field. Who's daring that big erasure,
that 'Not allowed'?

Walking with Anton

'If not here you'll find it nowhere.'
I hear only the last few words of what she said
as we walk the edge of the harbour and the moon –
as much as we see of it – lies on its back,
its enormous rind as if in some painting
of the kind we've learned to feel embarrassed
at liking to look at so much.

She was speaking, I think, of people
pretty much like ourselves, the strolling women,
the distracted fathers, the child whose mother
is thinking, without the least effort, it was
worth it, it was all worth it (although
quite what, she's forgotten), to watch the child
totter with the ocean close enough to stroke.

'You need only a few people and the moon,
and music from one of the cafés and laughter
across the water that may be mocking or may,
on the other hand, conceal utter heartbreak,
and we know our lives are in a story by Chekhov.'
I bite the leaf I've absently picked. I think,
'Is there no end to our pretentions?' I suppose I'm content.

Just a moment, do you mind?

Hey, that's not the bit I asked you
to remember, the black hulk of Bull Rock
and the moon lost completely when the clouds
came over –
                    it's earlier than that, the sea
in those twenty minutes tilted as silk's
tilted when it runs its currents, the moon
a word that veined us, the way we felt as we
watched it, more *real* you said than moon's
ever meant to be.
                    And what if it wasn't quite
so then, quite as I say it? It is now that it's said.

Come again?

I've watched again a movie I saw when I was seven.
The same trees thrashed, the same moon
glinted too brightly, the wrong people kissed,
a fat nurse with a nice voice turned out to be German.

I sat in an Auckland theatre, I think the St James.
I chewed a hole in a white silk scarf in special
wartime terror. There were wry British jokes that went
over my head. I think I remembered the bit

about the postman, but forgot two doctors thumping
each other because a nurse couldn't quite decide.
The hole in the gnawed scarf is the taste frightening
my mouth. When the trees pelt because that

is what studios knew scared everyone awfully,
especially ladies starting to run back home in the dark,
and the moon glitters so everything is knife-edge,
I am there in the dark as well, I am still not sure

who is really bad when everyone seems nice.
I watch the eyes slide above surgical masks.
I remember the balloon that goes limp when someone's dead.
All this time the detective's been looking after my scarf.

Love, assuming nothing

When she decided, 'All right then, *that's*
what you want,' left her jandals at the screen
door, hooked her bra on the doorknob

as she walked into the bunk room, the rest
of whatever she was wearing out there still
on the veranda, he quoted a poem

that said, 'Every gift I ever imagined
comes to me, love, on those naked feet,'
so that 'Smooth bastard' she responded,

but being as good as her word, the dawn's
there in no time. Then asked, 'That French
poet, right?', and he said, 'It was.'

'Then don't,' she told him. 'Next time you
come at that caper, the deal's called off.
Say it like it is or forget it.' He'd seldom

thrilled at anything so direct. He shoved
the *Collected Valéry* beneath the mattress.
Believe it or not, they lasted: as did 'every gift'.

Three's a crowd

We've looked together – what, three, four, times? –
at Manet's barmaid. Insolent? Not quite.
Nor melancholy either, her canny eye
for fetching decent tips from handsome cads.
'You'd have done it with like composure,' I tell
the woman I'd rather see there, pouring
thimbled absinthe, than Cleopatra
talking barge-talk, gold-hulled as you like.
'I rather fancy strolling in and simply ordering.'
A touch of boredom, an obliging nod.
We both, as it happens, are wearing black.
We look at the painting I love as much as any.
'This is as good as it gets,' isn't that too
what she thinks, that marvellous unflinching gaze?
She may well be thinking of children, some impending
grief. Or joy, don't leave that out, joy's
in there too. I want to touch her hand. Taste
the glimpse of her throat. Hit the phrase to set
her smiling. 'Imagine being at that bar,' the woman
I stand with tells me. 'Such loneliness surrounds her.
All those mirrors reflecting, both the world, and not.'
And her curious judgement: 'Wish I'd known Manet.'

On the odd eventful morning

joy's the word I want, and say it.
I think of those broad old-fashioned ties
men used to wear, wide across as a hand,
and a blazoned tie-pin too, 'Joy'
flashed out in metal when the man
puts his arm across his girl as she wants
to shriek, say, on the Big Dipper
he's more or less hassled her to go on.
'Joy' catches the sun, it's the shining
bar bent into a word across a big
bright tie, the kind there in a movie
I saw as a child, surprising how I think
of it this morning and am certain it's true,
just as joy's the word I'm after.
And then I remember a word from back
then too, it was on the killer's
tie-pin spelling out 'Bruno' I think
it may have been, on the steps of a huge
building in Washington, was it? The man
with the pin bent to glint out his name,
and so he was caught, the crime revealed,
justice done as it had to be done,
the girl dead in the Tunnel of Love
in the total story, which of course
I do not remember, but the shining
tie-pin for sure, the word there as he
turned that caught him. I remember that.

Skol

A man I talked with in a bar in Berlin
once read poetry, he said, with passion, served
with distinction in an army he loathed. Beyond
which he said little. He drank Schnapps. He advised,
as we parted, to avoid epiphanies as I would gunfire.
His phrase for ordering a Schnapps was 'to dim the lights.'

Sight unseen

A famous foreign poet came to the farm I lived on
in Pukeroro. He liked the name 'morepork' when it

narrowed the night to one insistent repetition,
he said – it was February – this was the perfect

place, surely, for fireflies, which at that time
I had never seen, not even in poetry.

A friend, a clever attractive woman, drove
him back to town. He said as they turned

to the main road near the Norfolk
pine, 'Do you mind if we ride in silence?

I intend to untangle what the stars down
here are up to.' He wrote a poem that perhaps

may or may not be about his visit, and the wine
we drank together, and the feeling I had as he stood

at the back veranda and looked intently as far
as a paddock of maize where, if you waited

with utter patience, you would hear the army
worm's destructive rustling, which I told him

of, and he smiled, it was like a smile
in a Bergman movie, you needed critics to explain.

The poem perhaps also spoke of how light is best
loved in tiny fragments, how stars can overdo it

when sky sprawls so many, how an owl
becomes a hooded pinprick at world's darkest end.

Any heart would give a leap

on meeting, as I do, a woman whose calling is to discourse
in the cleverest way on Theoretical Approaches
to Biographical Texts – a Chair being the diamond in her sights,
who regards the common reader pretty much as a terrier
assesses rodents from the perspective of how necks
are best snapped:
                            then to hear she jumps from aircraft
at 10,000 feet, that her hobby is precisely that,
to step from a rushing door into pure speculation,
to drop for the thrill of both utter and dangerous
freedoms:
                    that she grips for the hands of other
jumpers, forms one of those famous descending circles
photographers die for, a human plunging Stonehenge
you might think as gravity occurs:
                                        to hear
that, to meet her, to walk with this woman
who hates it that a sliver of discourse might drift away,
a tessera make off without standing to account,
yet has – I hear too from a colleague – a special
emergency chute she has hand-embroidered
with conventional prayer, a 'Lord be with Me'
reminder should the ground sprawl sudden
and quicker than expected, oh unravelling text. . . .

This is a puzzle I'm ill at ease with. This is 'a self
constructed from diverse fields of semantic force.'
There, I quote her, granting gouged respect.

After that, to begin with

The wind has talked through most of what
we have said together, the wind has cleared
its throat as though doing us a favour. We
wait the streaming of leaves to pile
the corners of the veranda, before we say,
'The wind we never would have believed
could last so long, has scarcely begun.'

Then proving us wrong, there is stillness
the shape of crystal slipped over the hollow
of the wind, a new fear, a different fear,
making us stand and look to trees
carved from something darker than darkness,
and we say, 'At least a few stars have made
it,' surprising us, the stars, our being

able to say, 'for certain', an exhilaration
which after all is our simply observing distance,
and giving it a name, and saying, 'There are
seven now that we count, seven,' which seems
an extraordinary thing to say, 'seven stars after
so much wind,' the silence laid like
a scythe against a wall for wind to dry.

First time, about Easter

There was a donkey inside a wire fence where the road
begins its first climb to the Rimutakas.

We passed it on Friday late afternoon for years,
passed it again coming back on Sundays, or thought

so in winter, when the dark was already down.
It was more grey than not, though children

reasonably argued the toss, and its muzzle
this frosty white, without question. You could not of course

hear from inside the car, but once we saw
its neck extended, its teeth displayed, without

doubt it was braying, and looked hurt: our driver
said No, it was nothing like it, yet thought of the horse

with the spiked tongue in *Guernica,* the blue-grey horse,
or paler even, imagine the glare of a search-light

picking it out in a show called 'War Arriving'.
Then one day it is gone, the donkey on the first

incline towards the Rimutaka hill. A dozen reasons.
I forgot, says another driver, a long time later,

to ever mention, did I, the one time
it snowed that far down the hill, the donkey

standing in the white paddock brought tears
to my eyes? Its head hung forward

as though too heavy for its body. As though,
finally and forever, that bit too much.

A donkey in a snowed-in paddock, under trees black as its hooves. On the Rimutaka road. One Friday.

Us, then

I see this photo of the lesula, the just-found
monkey in the Congo. He could be an Amish.
His whiskers frame a man. His human nostrils
decidedly close to home, so similar as we are.
His eyes remind me of my father. His intelligence
that comes from being shot at, and eaten.
There are fewer lesula left than people who read Swift.

Cliché winks across his shoulder. El Greco, someone
writes, anticipated Darwin with his hunch
about primates. The story already evolves
as we hold each other's gaze. He is spared the worst
excesses we gene-folk have got up to. He is
reticent, he harbours malice to no one, the prophet,
I would like to think, who has summed us up.

There are paintings too in Venice with monkeys
in their corners, Last Suppers with their cousins
watching the betrayal minutes before it comes,
the bread about to break into another story.
A monkey observing a man makes its hirsute point.
He knows I am raising a gun, I who have never
held one. I know, quite rightly, he expects the worst.

Saba's goat

So it was, the goat in the poem,
the goat in the paddock, its dry
bleat spoke for both . . .

every envy, every suffering,
the slow crackling munch
took in, thorn by thorn . . .

The sun bushed behind it,
each burning city, each victim's
wrack: how deftly human

tremor slots its eyes . . .
The mirror cracks in memory.
One by one we emerge.

Pre-nup, as they call it

The gradient too must be written in
    of the hill at whose crest love settles,
with a guarantee within reason of the weather
    once the confetti's thrown, the kettles
banged behind the honeymooning car.
A vow is naturally conditioned by how things are.

Finance, the equivalent of the rock
    on which JC established The Firm,
must be set in stone, as it were, fixed
    as Aorangi, as plaques in a berm
enclosure when the race is run.
(The point of the after-life too, 'The Will was done.')

Life being too promising to be harnessed
    with certainties of mere flesh or spirit,
Love, we will each declare, survives
    for so long as interest equals merit.
(The rational mind may erect its hut
even on the slopes, so to speak, of spontaneous rut.)

Yes, my love, we repeat, holding
    both balance and risk in equipoise,
medical know-how sensibly assures
    an equal number of daughters and of boys.
Perfection's not on the cards but close to it is.
That is what we sign up for. Any problem with this?

As one does, alas, cobber

It may just about be time to hand over.
It may pretty much be time to think clover
isn't likely to turn up the four favoured leaves
everyone who walks in summer secretly believes
is there somewhere, surely, exactly for him.
It may just about be time to accept that grim

quite as much as placid, as much as benign,
is the word that from now on tilts its sign
on the hill down to the river or the hill back up.
(One starts to remember such lines, 'Father, let this cup . . .')
Just about time, he repeats, certain at least
how the future tugs its moorings from the past.

We sit without saying much, glad the river
holds its calm, the long afternoon not over,
watching the flared west so casually ignite
the story the peaks reflect before the night,
before the night quite makes its stand, whatever
we take it to be, the odd star studding the river.

'It is the wind he hoped for . . .'

It is the wind he hoped for, an edge
of gale even on the dark veranda,
the moon thrashed through the branches,
the oil-drum behind the shed
at the southerly's urging boot. Even
love's the better for it, lips pressed
at her shoulder, the tile above the spare
bedroom's broken clap, telling him
too, *this is home, all right?*
The stacked logs in the old-fashioned
grate, the fierce irises take
along the resined pine, the walls
flag hot orange. 'In the cup
of the wind,' he says, 'what can't
we expect?' The house shakes like dice.